Krishna's Playful Pranks and Wisdom

Bibek Shah Shankhar

Bibek Shah Shankhar

© 2024, Bibek Shah Shankhar. All rights reserved.

No part of this publication may be reproduced, distributed, or transmitted in any form or by any means, including photocopying, recording, or other electronic or mechanical methods, without the prior written permission of the publisher, except in the case of brief quotations embodied in critical reviews and certain other noncommercial uses permitted by copyright law.

Contents

Chapter		1
1.	Chapter 1	3
	The Dawn Of Mischief in Vrindavan	
2.	Chapter 2	14
	The Great Butter Heist	
3.	Chapter 3	28
	The Enchanted Flute	
4.	Chapter 4	41
	The Misplaced Clothes	
5.	Chapter 5	52
	The Dance with the Ranclouds	
6.	Chapter 6	64
	The Taming of Kaliya	
7.	Chapter 7	76
	The Mysterious Fruit Seller	
8.	Chapter 8	87
	The Magical Mango Tree	

9.	Chapter 9	98
	The Festival of Colors	
10.	Chapter 10	110
	The Moonlit Dance	
11.	Chapter 11	122
	The Wisdom of Young Krishna	
12.	Chapter 12	134
	The Suset of Play and the Rise of Wisdom	
Thank you		145

Lets Start with This Maha mantra

Hare Krishna Hare Krishna,

Krishna Krishna Hare Hare,

Hare Rama Hare Rama,

Rama Rama Hare Hare

Chapter One

Chapter 1
The Dawn Of Mischief in Vrindavan

Chapter 1
The Dawn of Mischief in Vrindavan

CHAPTER 1

In Vrindavan's land, where the sun gently rose,
Lived young Krishna, with a charm that glows.
Birds sang sweetly, the river flowed with glee,
In this lush green world, as vibrant as could be

The peacocks danced, spreading feathers wide,
While Krishna watched, with eyes open wide.
He wore a crown of peacock feathers so bright,
And his smile shone like the moon at night.

The cows grazed peacefully in fields of green,
The happiest, most content herd ever seen.
Krishna would call, each by its name,
For he loved them all, each the same.

His flute lay silent, but not for long,
For Krishna's music was like a magical song.
When he played, the world seemed to pause,
Even the wind would stop to hear, without a cause.

CHAPTER 1

The village of Vrindavan, so simple and small,
Loved Krishna the most, young and tall.
His mother Yashoda, with love so deep,
Would gently smile, watching him leap

But where there's light, there's playful shadow,
And Krishna's pranks would soon follow.
He'd sneak into homes, with a mischievous grin,
Stealing butter, so smoothly, akin to the wind.

CHAPTER 1

"Krishna, Krishna," the villagers would call,
"Your pranks are known, by one and all."
But with a laugh and a dance, he'd escape,
Leaving behind, stories to shape.

In Vrindavan's heart, where tales intertwine,
Lived Krishna, where the stars align.
With each new dawn, his adventures began anew,
In the land of love, joy, and morning dew.

CHAPTER 1

So begins our tale, of magic and fun,
Of Krishna, the playful, mischievous one.
In the heart of Vrindavan, where dreams come alive,
With Krishna's pranks, where joy will thrive.

Chapter Two

Chapter 2
The Great Butter Heist

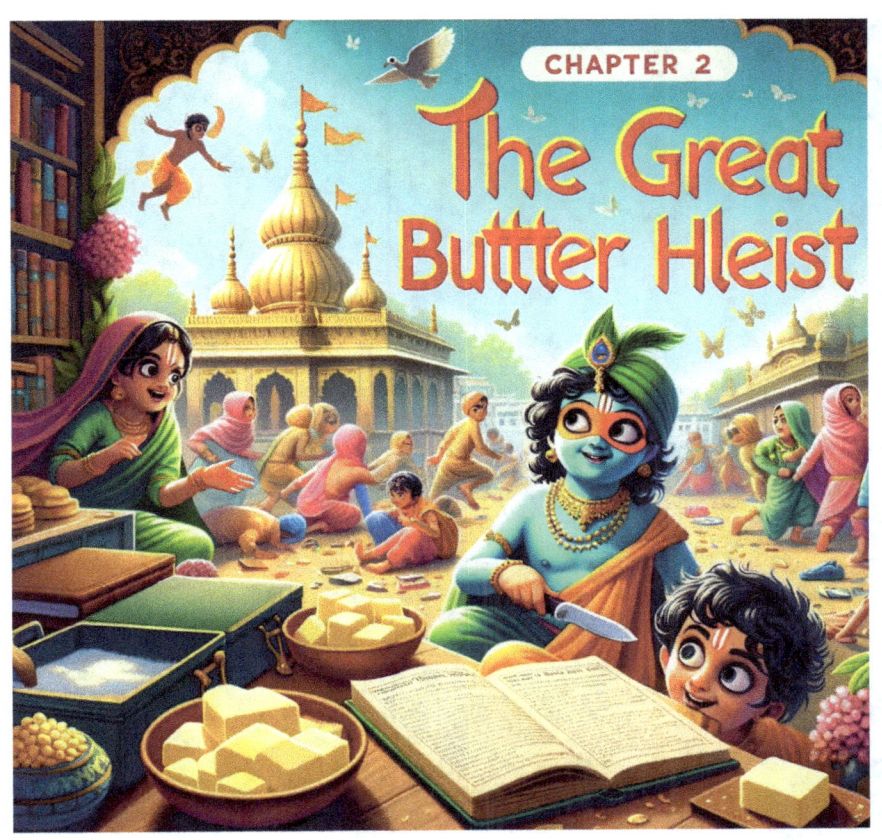

Chapter 2: The Great Butter Heist

In Vrindavan, under a sky so blue,
A plan was hatching, something new.
Krishna and friends, with a twinkle in their eye,
Dreamed up a heist, under the morning sky.

CHAPTER 2

"The butter jars," whispered Krishna with glee,
"Are full to the brim, as tasty as can be."
The village women made butter so sweet,
For Krishna and friends, it was the ultimate treat.

So begins our tale, of magic and fun,
Of Krishna, the playful, mischievous one.
In the heart of Vrindavan, where dreams come alive,
With Krishna's pranks, where joy will thrive.

They gathered in secret, a mischievous crew,
Balaram, Subala, and Sridama too.
They plotted and planned with whispers so light,
Ready for action, before daylight.

As the rooster crowed, and the village awoke,
Our band of friends, their silence broke.
With a laugh and a jump, they began their quest,
To steal the butter, and put their skills to the test.

They crept through the alleys, quiet as mice,
Avoiding detection, once, then twice.
With Krishna leading, so cunning and sly,
They reached the first house, under the sky.

Krishna stood tall, on his friends' stacked backs,
Reaching for the butter, avoiding all cracks.
His fingers dipped in, oh so slow,
And scooped out the butter, white as snow.

They moved through the village, house by house,
Silent as shadows, quiet as a mouse.
Each jar they found, they left slightly lighter,
Their hearts full of joy, their steps slightly brighter.

As the sun rose high, their adventure came to end,
With jars of stolen butter, around the bend.
They feasted on their prize, under a tree so tall,
Laughing and joking, having a ball.

But the village women soon found their jars bare,
And knew at once, who had been there.
"Krishna!" they exclaimed, shaking their heads,
But could not help smiling, free of any dreads.

For though he was mischievous, a prankster at heart,
Krishna's charm and joy were an integral part.
Of life in Vrindavan, so full of love and glee,
Where every day was a story, as sweet as could be.

So ended the tale of the Great Butter Heist,
With joy and laughter, not a single vice.
In Vrindavan's heart, where life danced and swirled,
Lived Krishna, the boy who enchanted the world.

Chapter Three

Chapter 3
THE ENCHANTED FLUTE

Chapter 3: The Enchanted Flute

In Vrindavan's heart, where whispers of wind play,
A story unfolded, one sunny day.
Krishna, the boy with eyes like the moon,
Decided to play a new tune, quite soon.

His flute, made of bamboo, simple and light,
Held songs of the stars, and the moonlit night.
When Krishna played, the world seemed to listen,
The waters stilled, and the leaves would glisten.

One morning, he wandered to the river's edge,
Sat under a tree, near the reeds and sedge.
He raised his flute, brought it close to his lips,
And played a melody that made time eclipse.

CHAPTER 3

The notes floated out, soft and clear,
Drawing all of Vrindavan near.
Cows paused in grazing, ears perked in delight,
Birds circled above, in a dance of flight.

The villagers stopped, their chores forgotten,
Caught in the spell of a tune begotten.
Children ran towards the melodious source,
Drawn to the music's enchanting force.

The peacocks fanned tails, in a vibrant display,
Dancing to the rhythm, in a joyful ballet.
Even the river seemed to slow its pace,
Captivated by the melody's grace.

Krishna played of mountains, of dreams and streams,
Of the quiet night and the moon's soft beams.
Each note a story, a whisper of the divine,
A symphony of nature, perfectly in line.

CHAPTER 3

The flute's magic wove a tapestry so rare,
Uniting all of Vrindavan in the open air.
It spoke of joy, of peace and of love,
Of the earth below and the sky above.

As the last note lingered, then faded away,
The spell gently broke, to the light of day.
The villagers smiled, hearts light and free,
Thankful for the moment, and the melody.

CHAPTER 3

Krishna's flute, a simple bamboo reed,
Had the power to enchant, a magical deed.
In Vrindavan's embrace, where life was a song,
The enchanted flute could do no wrong.

So ended the tale of the flute so divine,
Where each note played was a moment in time.
In Vrindavan, where dreams come to life,
The music still whispers, in joy and in strife.

Chapter Four

Chapter 4
The Misplaced Clothes

Chapter 4: The Misplaced Clothes

CHAPTER 4

In Vrindavan, where the sun warmly glows,
Unfolded a tale of misplaced clothes.
Krishna, the playful, with a spark in his eye,
Set out for a prank, under the open sky.

Near the river, where the waters run clear,
The village girls bathed, without any fear.
They left their clothes on the riverbank, neat,
As they played in the water, cooling their feet.

CHAPTER 4

Up in a tree, he climbed with a laugh,
Hiding their clothes, he awaited the aftermath.
The girls, none the wiser, continued their play,
Unaware of Krishna's prank underway.

As time passed by, they emerged to the shore,
Looking for clothes that were there no more.
Bewildered and shocked, they began to search,
While Krishna watched on, from his lofty perch.

"Krishna!" they called, sensing his ploy,
"Return our clothes, don't be so coy!"
Krishna just chuckled, his laughter rang clear,
"Promise to never bathe so near!"

The girls promised, their cheeks flushed with red,
Wanting nothing more than to be properly clad.
Krishna tossed down their clothes, his prank complete,
Leaving the girls to dress in haste, quite discreet.

CHAPTER 4

Though playful and cheeky, the lesson was kind,
To respect one's privacy and keep in mind,
That pranks can be fun, but should harm none,
And respect for others is second to none.

In Vrindavan, where life's lessons intertwine,
Krishna's pranks had a design so fine.
To teach and to guide, in laughter and light,
In this land of love, where hearts are bright.

So ended the tale by the river's flow,
Of Krishna, the prankster, with a radiant glow.
In Vrindavan's heart, where stories are sown,
The tale of the misplaced clothes is well known.

Chapter Five

Chapter 5
The Dance with the Ranclouds

Chapter 5: The Dance with the Rainclouds

In Vrindavan, where each day is a gift,
Came a time for spirits to lift.
The skies turned dark, the clouds gathered round,
Whispering the promise of rain's rhythmic sound.

Krishna, the joyful, with a gleam in his eye,
Watched the clouds gather in the sky.
He knew the dance of the rain was near,
A spectacle of nature, crystal clear.

He called to his friends, with a voice so bright,
"Come, let's dance with the clouds tonight!"
Under the sky, so vast and grand,
They formed a circle, hand in hand.

CHAPTER 5

The first raindrop fell, soft and light,
Like a silver pearl, shining bright.
Then more joined in, a symphony of drops,
In the dance of the rain, time simply stops.

Krishna began to dance, his feet so light,
Moving with the rain, pure delight.
Twirling and spinning, without a care,
His laughter mingled with the fresh wet air.

CHAPTER 5

The peacocks joined in, with feathers so fine,
Spreading their plumes in a colorful line.
The rhythm of the rain was their dance floor's beat,
In this monsoon celebration, joyously replete.

The villagers watched, hearts filled with glee,
At the sight of Krishna, wild and free.
Dancing with the rainclouds, a sight to behold,
In a world of colors, bold and untold.

CHAPTER 5

The rain washed the earth, fresh and new,
Leaving behind a world bathed in dew.
The fragrance of wet soil, so earthy and deep,
Brought promises of life, for the land to keep.

As the rain slowed, the sky cleared to blue,
Krishna's dance with the clouds, was almost through.
He smiled at his friends, his eyes shining bright,
In the land where rain brought pure delight.

CHAPTER 5

So ended the tale of the rain's embrace,
Of Krishna's dance, full of grace.
In Vrindavan, where every drop tells a story,
The dance with the rainclouds remains legendary.

Chapter Six

Chapter 6
The Taming of Kaliya

Chapter 6: The Taming of Kaliya

In Vrindavan's realm, where tales entwine,
Lived a serpent named Kaliya, in the Yamuna's brine.
His venom turned waters to a poisonous brew,
Causing fear and despair, through and through.

CHAPTER 6

Krishna, the brave, with courage so bright,
Decided to challenge Kaliya's might.
With a heart full of valor, pure and true,
He dove into the river, under skies so blue.

The waters churned, dark and deep,
As Kaliya awoke from his slumbering sleep.
With fangs that glistened, and eyes like coal,
The serpent faced Krishna, ready to patrol.

CHAPTER 6

The battle began, fierce and grand,
Between young Krishna and the serpent's stand.
Krishna, nimble and light on his feet,
Danced around Kaliya, avoiding defeat.

The villagers gathered, hearts filled with fear,
Praying for Krishna, whom they held so dear.
They watched in awe, as he fought with grace,
Determined to save Vrindavan's sacred space.

CHAPTER 6

Then Krishna leapt onto Kaliya's head,
And danced upon him, as the scriptures said.
With each step, he tamed the beast's pride,
Until Kaliya's venom was finally denied.

Kaliya bowed, his arrogance gone,
Realizing the battle, he had not won.
Krishna commanded, with a voice so clear,
"Leave these waters, let them be pure and dear."

The serpent slithered away, into the depths unseen,
Leaving behind waters, clear and clean.
The villagers cheered, their hearts alight,
For Krishna had won, the valiant fight.

The tale of the taming, spread far and wide,
Of how bravery and goodness can turn the tide.
In Vrindavan, where legends grow,
The story of Kaliya continues to glow.

CHAPTER 6

The sttory to lesssson for the conclusion of Vrindnavann ar a lessor oft courace, and sapat ace tohby Cor usttone do courage, compassion and starting a new.

So ends the chapter, with a lesson so true,
Of courage, compassion, and starting anew.
In the land of Vrindavan, so sacred and holy,
Krishna's tales are remembered, both humble and lofty.

Chapter Seven

Chapter 7
The Mysterious Fruit Seller

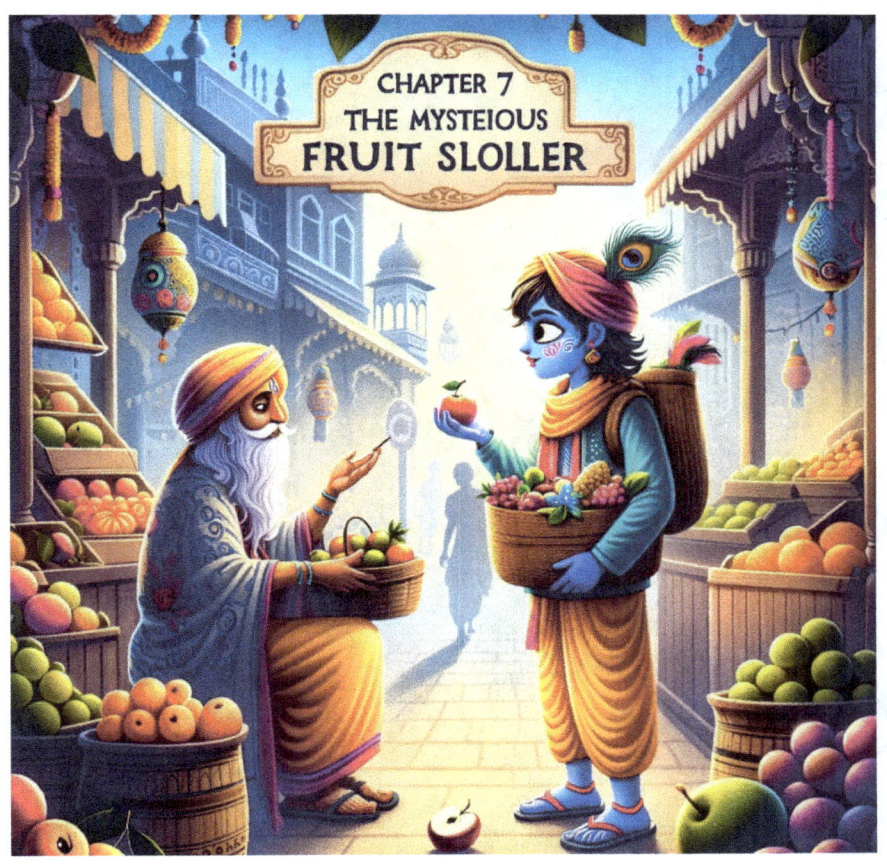

Chapter 7: The Mysterious Fruit Seller

In Vrindavan, where tales are spun,
A new adventure had just begun.
A fruit seller came to the town one day,
With baskets of fruits, in a colorful array.

CHAPTER 7

Her fruits were ripe, a sight to behold,
Glistening like jewels, red, green, and gold.
The villagers gathered, drawn by the sight,
Of mangoes, apples, and berries so bright.

Krishna, curious, joined the throng,
Amidst the laughter and the merchant's song.
He brought a handful of grains, so small and few,
Offering them with a heart so true.

The fruit seller smiled, her eyes kind and wise,
Seeing the offer as a precious prize.
She filled Krishna's arms with fruits galore,
Apples, bananas, and so much more.

But as she took the grains, a miracle occurred,
They turned to gold, without a word.
Her basket overflowed with shimmering light,
Turning her simple day to a magical night.

CHAPTER 7

The villagers gasped, amazed by the sight,
Of the grains turned gold, so shiny and bright.
Krishna just chuckled, a twinkle in his eye,
His playful nature, always sly.

The fruit seller, grateful, her heart full of joy,
Thanked Krishna, the mischievous boy.
She left the village, her heart light and merry,
Her life transformed, no longer weary.

CHAPTER 7

The tale of the fruit seller spread wide and far,
Of how kindness and generosity are the best by far.
In Vrindavan, where miracles abound,
The story of the mysterious merchant is found.

So ends the chapter of the generous exchange,
A reminder that life can be surprising and strange.
In the land of Vrindavan, with stories so tender,
The tale of the mysterious fruit seller we remember.

Chapter Eight

Chapter 8
The Magical Mango Tree

Chapter 8: The Magical Mango Tree

In Vrindavan's heart, where dreams take flight,
There stood an old tree, a pitiful sight.
Barren and dry, without a single leaf,
It stood all alone, in stark relief.

CHAPTER 8

The children would pass, not a glance they'd give,
For what joy could a lifeless tree give?
But Krishna saw more than just bark and branch,
He saw a chance for life to advance.

One sunny day, under the azure sky,
Krishna approached the tree, with a twinkle in his eye.
He touched its trunk, so gnarled and old,
And spoke softly, his voice brave and bold.

"O ancient tree, awaken from your sleep,
Let your roots go deep, where the earthworms creep.
Rise up from sorrow, embrace the light,
Bloom and grow, to a magnificent height."

The children watched, curious and still,
As a miracle unfolded, against the hill.
The tree trembled, its branches shook,
And the earth around, it gently took.

CHAPTER 8

Leaves sprouted green, unfolding like hands,
Reaching for the sun, over the lands.
Mangoes appeared, golden and sweet,
A luscious treat for the children to eat.

The children danced, their laughter rang,
Around the mango tree, they sang and sang.
Krishna smiled, his heart content,
At the joy and life the old tree lent.

CHAPTER 8

The tree stood tall, its branches wide,
A symbol of hope, with nothing to hide.
Birds came to nest, in its sturdy boughs,
Singing songs of joy, breaking all vows.

The tale of the tree spread near and far,
A story of hope, brighter than a star.
In Vrindavan, where miracles are seen,
The magical mango tree became a dream.

CHAPTER 8

So ends the chapter, with a message clear,
Of hope and rebirth, year after year.
In the land of Vrindavan, where legends are born,
The story of the magical mango tree is adorned.

Chapter Nine

Chapter 9
The Festival of Colors

Chapter 9: The Festival of Colors

In Vrindavan, a village of delight,
A festival approached, colorful and bright.
Holi, the festival of colors and joy,
Awaited each girl and every boy.

Krishna, with a plan, mischievous and keen,
Gathered his friends, not to be seen.
They mixed their colors, vibrant and bold,
Reds, yellows, purples, and blues untold.

The day dawned clear, a canvas so white,
Ready for colors to dance in the light.
The villagers emerged, dressed in attire plain,
Unaware of the impending colorful rain.

CHAPTER 9

With a shout of joy, Krishna led the charge,
Armed with colors, his palette large.
He flung the powder, high in the air,
A rainbow exploded, in the morning fair.

The air filled with laughter, shouts, and cheers,
As colors descended, on the villagers' ears.
Reds on cheeks, blues in hair,
Joyous chaos spread everywhere.

CHAPTER 9

Radha joined in, with a smile so wide,
Throwing colors with a playful stride.
Soon everyone was covered, from head to toe,
In a vibrant spectrum, a glistening glow.

They danced and sang, in the colored haze,
Celebrating Holi, in so many ways.
Drums beat rhythmically, feet tapped the ground,
In Vrindavan, happiness was found.

As the day waned, the colors dimmed,
Leaving memories, joyful and brimmed.
The villagers looked at each other and knew,
That the festival of colors had united their crew.

In Vrindavan, where stories are told,
The festival of Holi never grows old.
A time of unity, love, and fun,
Under the same bright, shining sun.

CHAPTER 9

So ends the tale of Holi's hue,
A festival of colors, for me and you.
In the heart of Vrindavan, where life is a song,
The festival of colors will always belong.

Chapter Ten

Chapter 10
THE MOONLIT DANCE

Chapter 10: The Moonlit Dance

In Vrindavan, beneath a moon so bright,
A dance was planned, deep into the night.
Krishna, the charmer, with a smile so wide,
Invited his friends to dance by his side.

CHAPTER 10

The moon shone full, a silver sphere,
Casting a glow on the land so dear.
The night was alive, with whispers of light,
Setting the stage for a magical sight.

Krishna took his flute, his companion true,
And played a melody, as the night wind blew.
Notes floated upwards, mingling with the stars,
A music so sweet, it healed all scars.

CHAPTER 10

The gopis gathered, hearts alight with glee,
Drawn to the sound, so enchanting and free.
They formed a circle, around Krishna they spun,
Dancing to the tune of the midnight sun.

Their feet tapped rhythms on the soft earth bed,
As they moved gracefully, led by the thread,
Of Krishna's melody, so profound and clear,
That it seemed the heavens themselves drew near.

CHAPTER 10

The peacocks strutted, their feathers unfurled,
Adding to the beauty of this wondrous world.
The trees swayed gently, in the moonlit trance,
As if they too wished to join the dance.

The dance went on, time lost its reign,
In the realm of joy, free from pain.
Under the moon, they twirled and leapt,
In a world where only love was kept.

CHAPTER 10

As dawn approached, the music slowed,
The night's enchantment gently stowed.
Krishna's flute whispered a soft goodbye,
Under the fading starlit sky.

The gopis departed, hearts full of song,
Knowing this night would stay with them long.
In Vrindavan, where dreams take flight,
The moonlit dance was a pure delight.

So ends the tale of the night so grand,
Where Krishna and friends danced hand in hand.
In the land of Vrindavan, where legends dance and prance,
Lives the memory of the moonlit dance.

Chapter Eleven

Chapter 11
The Wisdom of Young Krishna

Chapter 11: The Wisdom of Young Krishna

In Vrindavan, where stories weave and twine,
Lived Krishna, youthful and divine.
More than a prankster, with a mischievous smile,
His wisdom ran deep, profound and versatile.

CHAPTER 11

As the sun rose high, and the day began to unfold,
Krishna's words of wisdom were pure as gold.
To friends and villagers, he would often impart,
Lessons of life, straight from the heart.

"True strength," he said, "lies not in might,
But in standing for truth, for what is right."
He taught them to be brave, to be kind and wise,
To see the world through empathetic eyes.

CHAPTER 11

"Joy is found," Krishna would sing,
"Not in possessions, but in simple things."
He played his flute, a melody so sweet,
A reminder that in simplicity, life is complete.

Under a banyan tree, he once shared,
"Nature is a treasure, to be loved and cared.
Respect the earth, the sky, the sea,
For they are the keepers of mystery."

To a friend feeling low, Krishna gently spoke,
"Life is a play, don't let your spirit be broke.
Embrace each moment, be present, be true,
For each day is a gift, fresh and new."

As dusk fell, by the Yamuna's gentle flow,
Krishna's insights continued to glow.
"Unity and love," he reflected in the twilight,
"Are the forces that turn darkness into light."

Each word he said, each lesson he gave,
Was a ripple in the waters, a wave.
His wisdom, like an eternal, guiding star,
Illuminated paths, both near and far.

In Vrindavan, where stories are born and thrive,
Krishna's wisdom keeps the soul alive.
A young sage, a guide, a friend so dear,
In the heart of the village, ever near.

CHAPTER 11

So ends the chapter of wisdom so bright,
Shining through Vrindavan, day and night.
In the land where tales and truths entwine,
Lives the wisdom of young Krishna, timeless and divine.

Chapter Twelve

Chapter 12

THE SUSET OF PLAY AND THE RISE OF WISDOM

Chapter 12: The Sunset of Play and the Rise of Wisdom

In Vrindavan, where rivers of stories flow,
Comes a time of change, subtle and slow.
The sun sets on Krishna's days of youthful play,
As the horizon of wisdom lights his way.

CHAPTER 12

From mischievous pranks and joyful dance,
Emerges a sage's profound, insightful glance.
The boy who stole butter, who played with the herds,
Now speaks of life's truths, in profound words.

The village listens, gathered around,
Captivated by the wisdom profound.
Krishna, once the prankster, now the guide,
Shares insights where truth and love reside.

CHAPTER 12

"Life," he says, "is a journey, a sacred quest,
Filled with challenges, trials, and rest.
Embrace each chapter, each phase, each role,
For they are the steps towards the ultimate goal."

The cows he once tended, gaze with pride,
At the young boy who stood by their side.
Now a beacon of light, a source of inspiration,
A symbol of hope and divine aspiration.

The peacocks still dance, the river still flows,
But in Krishna's eyes, a deeper knowledge shows.
A transition from play to wisdom's embrace,
Marking a path for the human race.

In the twilight of play, as stars appear,
Krishna's laughter still echoes, clear and dear.
But now it's joined by a wisdom so deep,
Guarding Vrindavan, even in sleep.

CHAPTER 12

The sunset of play, a beautiful close,
Leads to a night where wisdom glows.
In the heart of the village, under the sky's dome,
Krishna's journey from boy to sage is known.

So ends our tale, in Vrindavan's embrace,
Of Krishna, who grew with grace and pace.
From playful pranks to wisdom's light,
He remains Vrindavan's eternal delight.

Thank you

www.ingramcontent.com/pod-product-compliance
Lightning Source LLC
Chambersburg PA
CBHW071349080526
44587CB00017B/3030